Find the Gifts

on The Twelve Days of Christmas

Illustrated by Jerry Tiritilli

Louis Weber, C.E.O.
Publications International, Ltd.
7373 North Cicero Avenue
Lincolnwood, Illinois 60646

Manufactured in the U.S.A.

8 7 6 5 4 3 2 1

ISBN 1-56173-164-1

PUBLICATIONS INTERNATIONAL, LTD.

On the **1st** day of Christmas my true love sent to me a partridge in a pear tree.

On the **2nd** day of Christmas my true love sent to me

2 turtle doves,

& a partridge in a pear tree.

Kringle's Nursery was having a sale on partridges in pear trees. But where do you suppose my true love found two turtle doves? (What is a turtle dove, anyway?)

MISTLETOE

SALE

PEPPERS

KRINGLE'S NURSERY

BUY YOUR CHRISTMAS PARTRIDGE NOW!

PUMPKINS
$5.00
$3.00
$1.00
FREE

MIXED NUT TREE

FAMILY TREE

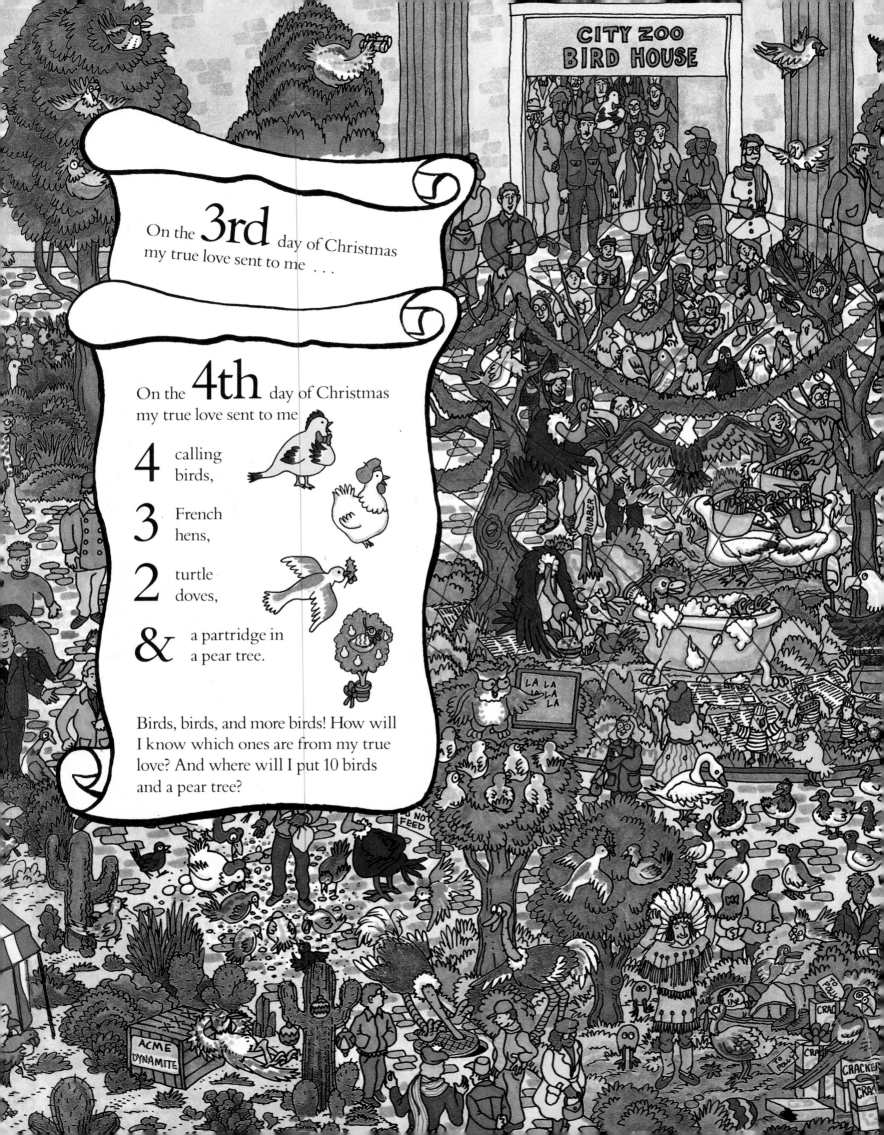

On the **3rd** day of Christmas my true love sent to me . . .

On the **4th** day of Christmas my true love sent to me

4 calling birds,

3 French hens,

2 turtle doves,

& a partridge in a pear tree.

Birds, birds, and more birds! How will I know which ones are from my true love? And where will I put 10 birds and a pear tree?

On the **5th** day of Christmas my true love sent to me

5 golden rings,

4 calling birds,

3 French hens,

2 turtle doves,

& a partridge in a pear tree.

Things look pretty crazy at S. Claus & Sons Department Store! I hope my true love didn't have to wait in a long line to buy my five golden rings.

On the **6th** day of Christmas my true love sent to me

6 geese a-laying,

5 golden rings,

4 calling birds,

3 French hens,

2 turtle doves,

& a partridge in a pear tree.

There's nothing like Christmas down on the farm. It is so peaceful and quiet. Or is it?

On the **7th** day of Christmas my true love sent to me

7 swans a-swimming,

6 geese a-laying,

5 golden rings,

4 calling birds,

3 French hens,

2 turtle doves,

& a partridge in a pear tree.

Christmas isn't all sleigh rides and snowflakes! In fact, my true love saw Santa playing a quick nine holes down in Florida this year!

On the **8th** day of Christmas my true love sent to me

8 maids a-milking,

7 swans a-swimming,

6 geese a-laying,

5 golden rings,

4 calling birds,

3 French hens,

2 turtle doves,

& a partridge in a pear tree.

Oh, my! What shall I do with all this milk? I think I shall churn it into butter and bake cookies!

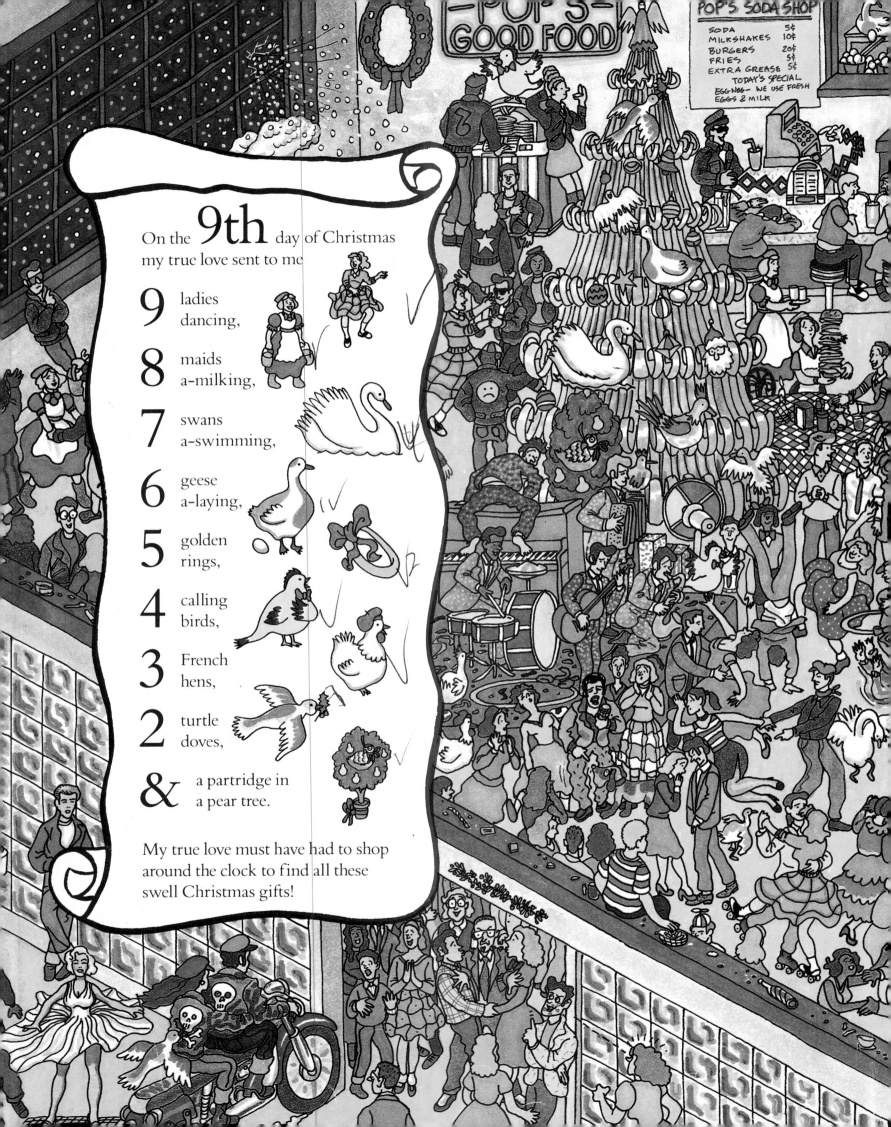

On the **9th** day of Christmas my true love sent to me

9 ladies dancing,

8 maids a-milking,

7 swans a-swimming,

6 geese a-laying,

5 golden rings,

4 calling birds,

3 French hens,

2 turtle doves,

& a partridge in a pear tree.

My true love must have had to shop around the clock to find all these swell Christmas gifts!

POP'S GOOD FOOD

POP'S SODA SHOP

SODA   5¢
MILKSHAKES   10¢
BURGERS   20¢
FRIES   5¢
EXTRA GREASE   5¢
    TODAY'S SPECIAL
EGGNOG— WE USE FRESH
EGGS & MILK

On the **10th** day of Christmas my true love sent to me

10 lords a-leaping

9 ladies dancing,

8 maids a-milking,

7 swans a-swimming,

6 geese a-laying,

5 golden rings,

4 calling birds,

3 French hens,

2 turtle doves,

& a partridge in a pear tree.

I'm going to need a bigger attic to hold all these lords and ladies and maids and . . . whew! My true love is going completely overboard this year!

PUNCH

On the **11th** day of Christmas my true love sent to me . . .

On the **12th** day of Christmas my true love sent to me

12 drummers drumming,

11 pipers piping,

10 lords a-leaping,

9 ladies dancing,

8 maids a-milking,

7 swans a-swimming,

6 geese a-laying,

5 golden rings,

4 calling birds,

3 French hens,

2 turtle doves,

& a partridge in a pear tree!

Whew! I would have been happy with a pair of mittens from my true love! Were you able to find all the gifts on the 12 days of Christmas? If you'd like to have even *more* fun, go back to each scene and find these other funny things!

Kringle's Nursery

- ☑ Peter Piper and his peck of pickled peppers
- ☐ George and his cherry tree
- ☐ A lemon that is not a fruit
- ☐ Pretty powerful mistletoe
- ☐ Two squirrels who are nuts
- ☐ A family tree
- ☐ A pumpkinhead
- ☐ Eve and the apple
- ☐ A shoe tree

City Zoo Bird House

- ☑ "A bird in the hand is worth two in the bush"
- ☐ Jail birds
- ☐ Two cans
- ☐ A proud peacock
- ☐ A bird bath
- ☐ Lovebirds
- ☐ An even balder eagle
- ☐ Blackbirds baked in a pie
- ☐ A rubber chicken

Candy Cane Farm

- ☑ The Ugly Duckling
- ☐ Baa, Baa black sheep . . .
- ☐ The farmer in the dell . . .
- ☐ Little Bo-Peep
- ☐ The cow jumped over the moon . . .
- ☐ Three Billy Goats Gruff
- ☐ Peter, Peter, pumpkin-eater . . .
- ☐ Three Little Pigs
- ☐ Little Miss Muffet
- ☐ Mary had a little lamb . . .

S. Claus & Sons Department Store

- ☑ Long John Silver
- ☐ A peeping Tom
- ☐ A pampered pet
- ☐ A "pool" table
- ☐ A powerful vacuum cleaner
- ☐ A customer who is "all washed up"
- ☐ A sleeping beauty
- ☐ "Strike!"
- ☐ A pair of diamonds